CONTENTS

CHAPTER 1

WHAT IS ROCK MUSIC?

Find a dictionary and look up the word "rock". It will say something like this:

A form of popular music with a strong vocal using guitar, drums and bass.

That's a correct but dull description.
And rock music is anything but dull.

Rock music is powerful and exciting.
Rock music is the way your heart beats faster and life seems better when you hear your favourite band.

THE STORY OF ROCK MUSIC

Steven Rosen

CLASH
by ticktock

Copyright © ticktock Entertainment Ltd 2009

First published in Great Britain in 2009 by ticktock Media Ltd,
The Old Sawmill, 103 Goods Station Road, Tunbridge Wells, Kent, TN1 2DP

project editor and picture researcher: Ruth Owen
ticktock project designer: Simon Fenn

Thank you to Lorraine Petersen and the members of nasen

ISBN 978 1 84696 945 4 pbk

Printed in China

Picture credits (t=top; b=bottom; c=centre; l=left; r=right):
Richard E Aaron/Redferns: 23. R BAMBER/Rex Features: 22. Paul Bergen/Redferns: 26, 28. Fin Costello/Redferns:
31. Deltahaze Corporation/Redferns: 6. GAB Archives/Redferns: 17t. Getty Images: 10-11, 13. iStock: OFC.
Elliott Landy/Redferns: 18-19. Gered Mankowitz/Redferns: 27. Chris Morphet/Redferns: 14t. Michael Ochs
Archives/Getty Images: 5r, 5l, 7, 9r, 12, 21. Popperfoto/Getty Images: 8, 14b. David Redfern/Redferns: 20. Lorne
Resnick/Redferns: 24. Ebet Roberts/Redferns: 25. Rolling Stones/GAB Archives/Redferns: 15.Shutterstock: 1, 2-3, 4-
5, 6-7 (background), 9l, 14 (background), 21 (background), 22-23 (background), 26 (background).
Time & Life Pictures/Getty Images: 16. WireImage: 29.

Every effort has been made to trace copyright holders, and we apologise in advance for any omissions. We would be
pleased to insert the appropriate acknowledgments in any subsequent edition of this publication.

Throughout rock's history, one group of musicians influenced the musicians that came after them.

But who are the most important musicians in rock's history?

Rock music fans will never stop arguing about this!

Buddy Holly was the first musician to use two guitars, bass and drums in his band.

Chuck Berry

CHAPTER 2

HOW IT ALL BEGAN

Rock and roll came from the mixing of country music and the blues.

The blues belonged to black musicians. It came from spirituals and songs sung by black farm workers.

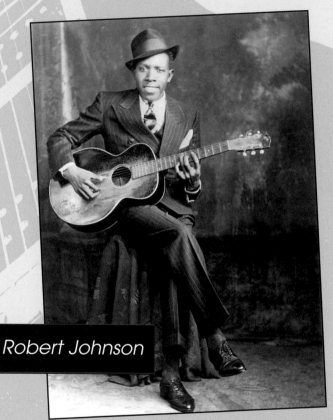

Robert Johnson

Robert Johnson was a gifted Delta blues guitarist.

Rock legend says that Johnson sold his soul to the devil to gain his talent. His song *Cross Road Blues* tells the story.

Johnson only recorded 29 songs. He died in 1938 when he was just 27.

Johnson's music would influence future musicians such as the Rolling Stones, Cream, and later Eric Clapton.

In the 1950s, parts of America suffered from segregation. Black and white communities were separated. Black people did not have the same rights as white people.

Gifted black musicians, such as Howlin' Wolf and Muddy Waters, could not get big record labels to listen to them.

So, small record labels formed such as King, Chess and Aladdin. They recorded blues musicians and presented their music to the world.

Muddy Waters recording at Chess

In the 1950s, musicians began mixing the blues and country music to create something new – rock and roll.

On 10 May, 1954, a band leader named Bill Haley, recorded a song. It was called *(We're Gonna) Rock Around the Clock.*

Many people think this was the first rock and roll song.

Bill Haley and the Comets

In 1954, rock and roll's first superstar arrived on the scene. Elvis Presley was a poor boy from Tupelo, Mississippi, USA.

No one had ever heard anything like Elvis before. Elvis was a white singer who sounded black.

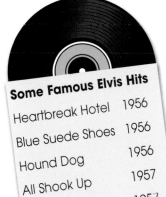

Some Famous Elvis Hits

Heartbreak Hotel	1956
Blue Suede Shoes	1956
Hound Dog	1956
All Shook Up	1957
Jailhouse Rock	1957

By the late 1950s, white audiences were listening to black rock and roll. They listened to artists such as Little Richard and Chuck Berry.

Elvis
*"The King"
Presley*

The electric guitar would be the main sound in rock and roll.

In the 1950s, companies such as Fender and Gibson began building electric guitars.

*Eric Clapton playing a later
model Fender Stratocaster*

Leo Fender and Les Paul created wonderful
guitars in tiny workshops.

CHAPTER 3

THE 1960s

Many people believe that the 1960s were the best time in rock and roll's history.

In California, USA, the Beach Boys were singing about surfers, the beaches, hot rod cars and young love.

The band used big vocal harmonies.

The Beach Boys

English bands such as the Yardbirds, the Animals and the Kinks were playing a type of English blues.

In Liverpool, England, four young musicians got together. They became The Beatles.

Liverpool is a port city. In the 1960s, local sailors were bringing back records from America.

The Beatles were influenced by American artists, such as Chuck Berry and Elvis. The Beatles were one of the first groups to write their own songs. Their vocals and vocal harmonies made every song fresh and different.

John Lennon

Paul McCartney

Ringo Starr

George Harrison

The Who were an English band. They came out of a movement called "the Mods".

The Mods were English teenagers. They drove scooters and wore the latest fashions from London.

The Who's sound was built around the songs and guitar playing of leader Pete Townshend.

Townshend became famous for smashing up his guitars on stage.

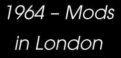

1964 – Mods in London

14

The Rolling Stones were another English band that listened to American blues.

Singer Mick Jagger and guitarist Keith Richards created a sound that was much bluesier than The Beatles.

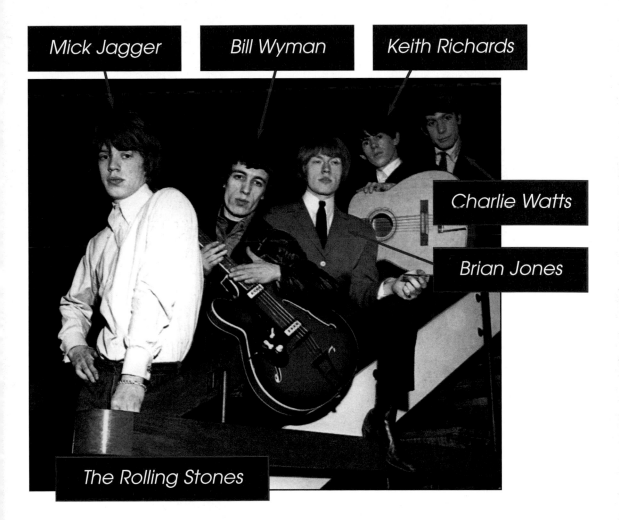

Mick Jagger

Bill Wyman

Keith Richards

Charlie Watts

Brian Jones

The Rolling Stones

In America, the Byrds combined folk music, jazz, American Indian music and country music.

The Byrds were one of the first rock and roll bands to come from the folk scene.

By the late 1960s, American bands were trying out different styles of music.

Bands such as Love, Spirit, The Doors and Buffalo Springfield were turning folk rock into psychedelic rock.

Psychedelic rock had a very dreamy feel to it. It mixed many music styles, from electronic music to music from India.

Jim Morrison, the lead singer of The Doors

In 1967, the Vietnam War was raging.

Many young people were anti-war. They wanted a new way to live that promoted love and peace. Many young people became "hippies". They listened to psychedelic rock bands such as Quicksilver Messenger Service and Jefferson Airplane.

Hippies

In the late 1960s, guitar players were beginning to take the electric guitar to new limits. They used effects such as fuzz and wah-wah pedals. The "Guitar Hero" was born.

Guitar Heroes

- Jeff Beck (The Jeff Beck Group)
- Eric Clapton (Cream)
- Jimmy Page (Led Zeppelin)
- Ritchie Blackmore (Deep Purple)
- Peter Green (Fleetwood Mac)
- Mick Taylor (Rolling Stones)
- Robin Trower (Procol Harum)
- Paul Kossoff (Free).

Jimi Hendrix was a gifted,
American guitarist.

Hendrix had been a back-up guitarist
for Little Richard. But Little Richard
would not give Hendrix a chance.
He could see how good he was!

So, Hendrix moved to England.

The English loved Hendrix
and turned him into a true
guitar legend.

He died at 27 from a
drug overdose.

18

CHAPTER 4

THE 1970s

In the 1970s, heavy metal bands created huge walls of sound by turning amplifiers up to ten!

Jimmy Page was a studio guitarist. He wanted to put together a band to rule the world.

Led Zeppelin were that band. They wrote amazing songs and were gifted musicians.

Led Zeppelin's *Stairway to Heaven* is so well-known that hundreds of radio stations play it every day.

Robert Plant

Jimmy Page

Led Zeppelin

Heavy Metal Greats

- Black Sabbath
- Deep Purple
- Aerosmith
- Alice Cooper
- Van Halen
- Mountain
- Grand Funk Railroad

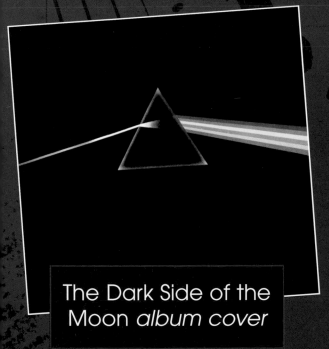

The Dark Side of the Moon *album cover*

Progressive rock bands, such as Pink Floyd, were also emerging.

Progressive rock was more complex than normal rock. Bands used bits of classical music. They used keyboards to create the sounds of instruments such as violins and horns.

In March 1973, Pink Floyd released *The Dark Side of the Moon*. The album stayed on the US charts for 14 years!

Bands such as the Sweet and T. Rex wore sequins, satin, make-up and six-inch heels.

David Bowie puts on Ziggy Stardust make-up

David Bowie used pop and even theatre in his music.

He turned himself into different characters, such as Ziggy Stardust and the Thin White Duke.

Then, in 1974, a new style of rock music was born in London – punk rock.

The guitars were out of tune. There were no melodies.

Sometimes the singer was singing one song while the band played another. Punk rock was anti-music!

England's Sex Pistols and The Clash were the most popular punk groups.

Johnny Rotten of the Sex Pistols

CHAPTER 5

THE 1980s

On 1 August, 1981, MTV (Music Television) came on the air.

Musicians were now making videos to promote their music. A band's "look" was as important as their sound.

Eddie Van Halen

Bands such as Bon Jovi, Mötley Crüe and Van Halen all looked great on TV. Their music became known as "hair metal" or "glam metal".

Guitarist Eddie Van Halen was a true guitar master. Every other player around was in awe of him.

In England, heavy metal groups such as Def Leppard, Iron Maiden and Saxon emerged.

Their music was called the New Wave of British Heavy Metal (NWOBHM).

Iron Maiden

In the 1980s, the Irish band, U2, had a major impact on rock music. Their music was built around the voice and songs of Bono, and the unique guitar sounds of The Edge.

CHAPTER 6

THE 1990s

In the cloudy, rainy city of Seattle, USA, "grunge" was born.

Grunge was a little bit punk, a little bit heavy metal.
Grunge musicians wore shabby clothes.
Their songs were usually about being unhappy.

Many people thought the grunge band Nirvana
were the "Great New Thing". Singer Kurt Cobain
was compared to John Lennon.

However, on April 5, 1994, Cobain killed himself.

*Kurt Cobain (centre)
with Nirvana in 1991*

Oasis

In the UK, "Britpop" bands brought back the sounds of The Beatles, the Rolling Stones and the Kinks.

The songs were catchy and you could sing along to all the lyrics.

Britpop bands
- Oasis
- The Verve
- Radiohead
- Suede
- Pulp
- Blur

CHAPTER 7

ROCK TODAY

Today, the rock music of the past continues to influence new musicians.

Thrash metal bands, such as Mastodon and Slipknot, have been influenced by Led Zeppelin, Black Sabbath and Iron Maiden.

Radiohead are a modern-day Pink Floyd.

Bands such as The Killers, Interpol and the Editors are taking the punk rock of the 1970s and turning it into something new.

2008 – the Editors play the Pinkpop Festival in Holland

Grunge has become post-grunge with bands such as the Foo Fighters, Collective Soul and Seether.

KT Tunstall

Female artists such as KT Tunstall, Alanis Morissette and Gwen Stefani have been influenced by lots of styles of music, including punk.

Who will be the rock greats of the future?
Will your favourite band be remembered in ten years?

NEED TO KNOW WORDS

amplifier A piece of equipment that makes sounds louder. An electric guitar is plugged into an amplifier.

bass A sound that is low and booming. A type of electric guitar with four strings and a lower sound than a normal electric guitar.

country music A style of American music that began in the 1940s. It was originally played by poor, white musicians. It mixed little bits of the blues and folk music.

Delta blues Blues music played by musicians in the Mississippi Delta area.

folk music A simple style of music usually played by a single singer with a guitar. The songs are about the life of the singer and their community. Folk songs were a way of passing along history.

fuzz A piece of equipment used with an electric guitar to make a fuzzy sound. The musician operates the equipment using a pedal.

heavy metal A style of music with loud guitars and big amplifiers. The singing style is almost like screaming.

influence When one thing shapes or has an effect on something else.

legend A story that is passed down through history and may be partly true and partly made up. Also, a person who has done something great and is remembered through history.

lyrics The words of a song.

record label A record company.

spirituals Religious folk songs that were first sung by black slaves in America.

Vietnam war A war in Asia between South Vietnam and North Vietnam. The war lasted from 1954 until 1975. America joined the war to help the South Vietnam army.

vocal The singing part of a song.

vocal harmony A singing part of a song that is different to the main vocal but blends with it to create a new sound.

wah-wah pedal A piece of equipment used with an electric guitar to make a sound like crying. The musician operates the equipment using a pedal.

MoRE ROCK STYLES

- **New Wave** – In the late 1970s, bands such as Blondie, Talking Heads and The Police smoothed the edge off of punk. They turned it into a music style that more people could enjoy and buy. This music was known as New Wave.

- **Goth rock** – The Cure played goth rock. They dressed up in black and looked like vampires.

- **Garage rock** – This style of music was played and recorded in garages in the 1960s. Today, it's back with bands such as The Hives and the White Stripes.

- **College rock** – This music grew up on college campuses across the USA, and in the UK. College rock was a little bit punk and a little bit New Wave – but it had a lot more melody. Bands include XTC, Edie Brickell and the New Bohemians, 10,000 Maniacs and R.E.M.

The Cure

ROCK MUSIC ONLINE

Websites

http://www.thebeatles.com/core/home/
A website all about The Beatles

http://www.trouserpress.com
Find out about alternative (different) styles of rock

INDEX

10,000 Maniacs 31

A
Aerosmith 21
Animals, the 12

B
Beach Boys, the 12
Beatles, The 13, 15
Beck, Jeff 17
Berry, Chuck 5, 9, 13
Black Sabbath 21, 28
Blackmore, Ritchie 17
Blondie 31
blues 6-7, 8, 12, 15, 30
Blur 27
Bon Jovi 24
Bono 25
Bowie, David 22
Britpop 27
Buffalo Springfield 16
Byrds, the 15

C
Clapton, Eric 6, 10-11, 17
Clash, The 23
Cobain, Kurt 26
Collective Soul 29
college rock 31
Cooper, Alice 21
country music 8, 30
Cream 6, 17
Cure, The 31

D
Deep Purple 17, 21
Def Leppard 25
Doors, The 16

E
Edge, The 25
Edie Brickell and the
   New Bohemians 31
Editors, the 28

F
folk music 15, 16, 30
Foo Fighters 29

G
garage rock 31

glam (hair) metal 24
glam rock 22
Green, Peter 17
grunge 26, 29
guitar heroes 17, 18
Grand Funk Railroad 21

H
Haley, Bill 8
heavy metal 25, 30
Hendrix, Jimi 18-19
Hives, The 31
Holly, Buddy 5
Howlin' Wolf 7

I
Interpol 28
Iron Maiden 25, 28

J
Jefferson Airplane 17
Johnson, Robert 6

K
Killers, The 28
Kinks, the 12, 27
Kossoff, Paul 17

L
Led Zeppelin 17, 20, 28
Lennon, John 13, 26
Little Richard 9, 18
Love 16

M
Mastodon 28
Morrison, Jim 16
Mötley Crüe 24
Mountain 21

N
New Wave 31
Nirvana 26

O
Oasis 27

P
Page, Jimmy 17, 21
Pink Floyd 25, 28
Police, The 31

post-grunge 29
Presley, Elvis 9, 13
progressive rock 21
psychedelic rock 16-17
Pulp 27
punk rock 23, 28, 31

Q
Quicksilver Messenger
   Service 17

R
R.E.M. 31
Radiohead 27, 28
rock and roll 8-9
Rolling Stones, the 6, 15, 17
Rotten, Johnny 23

S
Saxon
Seether 29
Sex Pistols 23
Slipknot 28
Stefani, Gwen 29
Suede 27

T
Talking Heads 31
Taylor, Mick 17
thrash metal 28
Trower, Robin 17
Tunstall, KT 29

U
U2 25

V
Van Halen 21, 24
Van Halen, Eddie 24
Verve, The 27

W
Waters, Muddy 7
White Stripes, the 31
Who, The 14

X
XTC 31

Y
Yardbirds, the 12

32